Grandparent Poems

Grandparent Poems

Compiled by John Micklos, Jr. • Illustrations by Layne Johnson

Wordsong

Boyds Mills Press

To grandparents everywhere, for all the joy they bring us
—J. M., Jr.

For the Johnsons, Megasons, Hudsons, and Hembrees . . . fond memories.
Special thanks to Emma, Mollie, Debbie and Stephen, Brett, Obie and Avis,
Shirley, Kevin, Eric, Saman and Steven, Harold, Maudie, Carolyn and Kelsey,
Elaine, Lauren, and Betty
—L. J.

Collection copyright © 2004 by John Micklos, Jr.
Illustrations copyright © 2004 by Layne Johnson

Published by Wordsong
Boyds Mills Press, Inc.
A Highlights Company
815 Church Street
Honesdale, Pennsylvania 18431
Printed in China

Publisher Cataloging-in-Publication Data (U.S.)

Micklos, John, Jr.
Grandparent poems / compiled by John Micklos, Jr. ;
illustrations by Layne Johnson.—1st ed.
[32] p. : col. ill. ; cm.
Includes index.
Summary: Poems in celebration of grandparents.
ISBN 1-56397-900-4
1. Grandparents—Poetry. 2. Poetry. I. Johnson, Layne. II. Title.
808.819/ 352 21   2004   AC   CIP
2001094549

First edition, 2004
The text of this book is set in 15-point Berkeley.

Visit our Web site at www.boydsmillspress.com

10 9 8 7 6 5 4

Contents

Grandmas and Grandpas

My grandma's face is rosy red;
She wears a scarf around her head;
And when she tucks me into bed,
She plants three kisses on my head.

And in the spring she always makes
A garden which she hoes and rakes;
She rubs my tummy when it aches
And bakes me special birthday cakes.

My other grandma's face is pale;
She sends me letters in the mail;
She taught me how to play the scale,
And once she wrote a fairy tale.

She knits me mittens, scarves, and socks;
She helps build castles with my blocks;
And when I got the chicken pox,
She let me have her button box.

My grandpa's fat but not too fat;
He likes to wear a cowboy hat;
He tells my grandma's cat to scat
(My grandma doesn't much like that).

He tells me stories that are true
Of all the things he used to do;
Sometimes he takes me to the zoo;
He's teaching me to yodel, too.

My other grandpa's thin and tall,
Which makes him good at basketball.
He visits us each spring and fall
And takes me walking in the mall.

We pick out things we'd like to own,
Like sailboats or a saxophone;
And when we're tired to the bone,
He treats me to an ice-cream cone.

—Mary Ann Hoberman

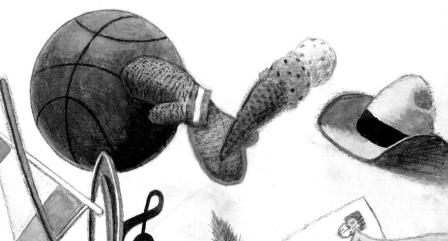

I Like to Walk with Grandma

I like to walk with Grandma.
  She shows me
      the different colors
      inside the neighbor's flowers—
      the ones that weren't there
         a minute ago.

I like to walk with Grandma.
  She stops
      and ties my shoe
      and won't make me
      do it all by myself.

I like to walk with Grandma.
  I hold her hand,
      and it's cool and soft
      and the wrinkles of her knuckles
      stay where I move them
      and she never says,
         "Stop that."

One time
  we skipped
  all the way
         to the corner.

—Jane Medina

Buddies

When Grandpa winks,
I wink.
When he giggles,
I giggle.
When his tummy
Feels rumbly,
My tummy
Feels rumbly.
I don't know how Grandpa
Got to be
So much like me,
But he is.
Maybe he's old enough
To act my age,
Maybe I'm young enough
To act his.

—David L. Harrison

Grandpa's Hands

Grandpa's hands are cracked and calloused,
Rough in every way,
From milking cows and fixing plows,
From stacking bales of hay.

Grandpa's hands are firm and strong,
His grip just like a vise,
From stringing wires and changing tires
In wind and rain and ice.

Yet Grandpa's hands are gentle.
It amazes me so much
That hands so rough and weathered
Could have such a gentle touch.

—John Micklos, Jr.

Pineapple Surprise

Grandma wasn't much for hugging.
She was entirely too frail
to give me piggyback rides
and moved too slow
for hide-and-seek.
But, sometimes,
while I played alone,
she would magically appear
with pineapple upside-down cake,
which took considerable time to make:

Honey-glazed pineapple rings
clinging to the bottom—
or was it the top?
Maraschino cherries pop-
ping with tooth-tingling
tangy sweetness,
two thick layers of buttery,
gooey, scrumptiously chewy,
pineapple-licious yellow cake
baked for nobody else but me.

—*Nikki Grimes*

In Grandpa's House

Long ago
when I was small
Grandpa wrote
upon the wall
and measured me
from toe to head
with shiny silver
lines of lead.
He marked each year,
he marked my growth,
and next to every line
he wrote:
Becca's five
or Becca's eight,
then he scribbled in
the date.
His hand was strong,
the markings clear;
"I love you" etched
from year to year
as inch by inch
was marked in time
with thin-as-tinsel
pencil lines,
charting days
when I was small. . . .
in Grandpa's house,
on Grandpa's wall.

—Rebecca Kai Dotlich

Grandpa's Sports Car

Grandpa has a sports car,
A bright-red racing sports car
With headlight eyes that open
At Grandpa's magic touch.

Grandpa takes me riding,
And sometimes when it's warm
He rolls the car top down
As we race along the road.

Then Grandpa says, "Hey, sport,
Let's stop for ice-cream floats."
And when the ride is over,
The top goes up, the headlights close,
And the sports car goes to sleep.

—John Micklos, Jr.

Welcome, Florence

She is our new grandmother,
What shall we call her?
Grandma?
But our old one looks down
    blinking like a star
      we still orbit.
What shall we call her?
Her own name, ma says,
that names a great city of art,
that gathers flowers, kindness,
grace into a fragrant bouquet.
Florence, we say, wearing gardenias,
Florence as if she were paintings
    we made ourselves
      and cherished.

—Judith W. Steinbergh

My Granddaddy
Is My Daddy Too

Nobody has a granddaddy
Like my granddaddy.
Nobody's granddaddy
Is named Douglas Jasper Blue.
Nobody's grandfather
Has smoked a pipe for fifty years
And always has tobacco to chew.
Nobody else's big daddy
Can carve whistles out of wood.
Nobody's else's grandfather
Has feet almost two feet long.
Only my grandpa
Can catch fifteen fish in a day.
And he makes up his very own silly songs.

Nobody has a granddaddy
Like my granddaddy.
I'm so lucky
That he's my one and only Daddy.

—Dinah Johnson

14

Big Mama

Big Mama is my grandmother.
She lives down south.

When we go to visit her
we eat grits and sausage and
pork chops and eggs for breakfast,
and we get up real early.

Big Mama has a great big yard
and a swing on her porch.

Big Mama has a dog that catches
rabbits and at night
the stars are very bright.

—Karama Fufuka

When Grandpa Reads to Me

I love to climb in Grandpa's lap
To hear my favorite books.
He reads the words and talks about
The pictures as I look.

Adventures flow from every page
When Grandpa reads the tales
Of pirates roaming on the seas
And ships with golden sails.

The characters can spring to life
Like Peter Pan and Pooh,
Madeline and Curious George
And Peter Rabbit, too.

Grandpa even does the voices.
I laugh until I'm weak
When I hear Grandpa's deep, low voice
Do Piglet's high-pitched squeak.

There's nothing I can't do through books.
There's nothing I can't see.
The whole world opens up its arms
When Grandpa reads to me.

—*John Micklos, Jr.*

16

Granny Granny Please Comb My Hair

Granny Granny please comb
my hair
you always take your time
you always take such care

You put me on a cushion
between your knees
you rub a little coconut oil
parting gentle as a breeze

Mummy Mummy
she's always in a hurry-hurry
rush
she pulls my hair
sometimes she tugs

But Granny
you have all the time
in the world
and when you're finished
you always turn my head and say
"Now who's a nice girl"

—*Grace Nichols*

17

Summer Twilight

Supper's over
Chores are done
Front porch swims
In setting sun
Rockers beckon
Tea is cold
Children gather
Good as gold
Eight o'clock
The house clocks chime.
Grandpa says:
It's story time.

—Eileen Spinelli

Night Walk with Grandpa

We walk home at night
from the meeting hall,
moon and stars
our only lights.
Rocky stone roads
pinch my sandaled toes;
Grandpa and I
hurry along.

I stare at shadows
moving through the trees
like scary monsters
glaring down at me.
I shudder and cling
close to Grandpa,
feeling safe as we
hurry home.

—Monica Gunning

I keep a photo of my Grandmother.
I have never seen my Grandmother.
I keep a photo of her
in my rose box.
My Grandmother
sitting on a chair
in the garden.

—*Sau Yee Kan*

The Picture

My Grandpa can't hear things as well as he used to,
He wears thick glasses to help him see.
When we ride in his car, he drives very slowly.
I feel his hand shake when he walks with me.

My Dad has a box that's filled with old pictures,
In some of them Grandpa's as young as my Dad.
There's one where he's holding my Dad on his shoulders,
When I see that picture, sometimes I feel sad.

My Grandpa's not strong but he's kind and he's funny,
Still I know he'll never be younger again.
So sometimes I wish I could climb in that picture
And visit with Grandpa the way he was then.

—*Jeff Moss*

My Grandma's Songs

would follow
the beat of
the washing machine

turning
our kitchen
into a dance floor

consoling
the chairs placed
upside down

delighting
the family portraits
on the walls

putting to sleep
the sheets
on the clothesline

giving flavor
to the boiling pot
of beans

the songs
my grandma
used to sing

could make
the stars
come out

could turn
my grandma
into a young girl

going back
to the river
for water

and make her
laugh and cry
at the same time

—Francisco X. Alarcón

Grandma Louise's Gingerbread

Grandmama made gingerbread—
her writing's on this card—
her recipe in curled black script
directs, "Don't beat too hard."

My mother ate it after school
cut in a warm brown square
when she was just a little girl,
and Grandmama was there.

Sugar, egg, and buttermilk,
molasses, ginger, flour—
mix and measure, put to bake
only half an hour.

I never met my grandmama
and never will (she's dead),
but I kind of know her, since
I eat her gingerbread.

—Crescent Dragonwagon

I Only Know the Stories

I never knew my grandfathers.
They died before I was born.
I only know them by the stories
That my family tells about them.

I never knew my father's father.
I only know the stories—
He left his plow in the field one day
On his tiny farm in Slovakia,
Sold the oxen and used the money
To make his way to America
In search of a better life.

I never knew my father's father.
I only know the stories—
He settled in Schenectady, New York,
Working in a factory by day and delivering newspapers
Each morning before dawn to support his growing family.
And he died young, too young, worn out
From working too hard, too long.

24

I never knew my mother's father.
I only know the stories—
He owned a farm in Delaware,
Raising cows and chickens, corn and wheat.
He worked in the fields all day
Through wind and rain and blazing sun,
Making a living, making a life.

I never knew my mother's father.
I only know the stories—
He became a state senator, respected by all.
At last he sold the farm and moved
To a fine house in the city,
And he died in a car crash
Just days before I was born.

I never knew my grandfathers.
I really wish I had.
But I'm glad I know about them
Through their stories.

—*John Micklos, Jr.*

Still

there

on your chair
my
one-eyed
tattered
teddy bear.

Still
there

on your chair

the book
you were reading
that night
to me

the bookmark
still tucked
to
page thirty-three.

Still
there

on your chair
your knitting needles
berry-blue—

a half-made
mitten
for
me
from you.

Your chair
is still—
but
it's still there.

Your pillow
smells
of
perfumed hair.

I *see*
your smile.

I *feel*
your touch.

I miss you so
so
so
so
much.

I miss you
morning,
noon,
and night.

I love you,
Grandma.

Good-bye.

Sleep tight.

—*Lee Bennett Hopkins*

I Remember Grandma

remembering
Grandma filling up this porch
with laughing
and stories about when
Mama was a little girl
and Grandma would hug me
and say
I was her very special own granddaughter.
But now she's gone.
I miss her—

        —*Nikki Grimes*

I remember Grandma's hair,
the flowered dress she'd always wear,
her squeaky wooden rocking chair.
I remember Grandma.

I remember Grandma's eyes,
so blue they sparkled like the skies,
the way she sang me lullabies.
I remember Grandma.

I remember Grandma's smell,
the flowery scent I knew so well,
the stories that she used to tell.
I remember Grandma.

I remember Grandma's touch,
those gentle hands I loved so much,
the locket she would always clutch.
I remember Grandma.

I remember Grandma's kiss.
That's the one thing I most miss.
I think of Grandma in Heaven above.
When I think of Grandma, I think of love.

        —*John Micklos, Jr.*

About the Poets

Francisco X. Alarcón is an educator and a poet who has written several poetry books for children, some published both in English and Spanish. His poem in *Grandparent Poems* comes from his book *Laughing Tomatoes and Other Spring Poems*.

Rebecca Kai Dotlich's poems have appeared in many children's magazines and in several anthologies. Her poetry books for children include *Sweet Dreams of the Wild* and *Lemonade Sun and Other Summer Poems*.

Crescent Dragonwagon is the author of many children's books, including *Home Place* and *Alligator Arrived with Apples: A Potluck Alphabet Feast*.

Karama Fufuka has written many poems and stories for children. Her contribution to *Grandparent Poems* comes from her book *My Daddy Is a Cool Dude*.

Nikki Grimes has published poems, articles, essays, editorials, and photographs in many national markets. She has written several books for young people, including *Something on My Mind*.

Monica Gunning's poems often reflect her childhood experiences in Jamaica. Her books include *Not a Copper Penny in Me House: Poems from the Caribbean* and *Under the Breadfruit Tree: Island Poems*.

David L. Harrison is the author of several popular poetry and picture books for children. His works include *Somebody Catch My Homework* and *A Thousand Cousins: Poems of Family Life*.

Mary Ann Hoberman is the author of many books for children. Her works include the award-winning book *A House Is a House for Me* and *Fathers, Mothers, Sisters, Brothers: A Collection of Family Poems*.

Lee Bennett Hopkins is one of the world's best-known poets and anthologists. His numerous books include the autobiographical *Been to Yesterdays: Poems of a Life*, from which his poem for this book comes.

Dinah Johnson, a university professor, has written several books for children, including *Sunday Week* and the poetry book *Sitting Pretty: A Celebration of Black Dolls*.

Sau Yee Kan's moving poem "I keep a photo of my Grandmother" comes from the book *Mother Gave a Shout: Poems by Women and Girls*, edited by Susanna Steele and Morag Styles.

Jane Medina has taught elementary school for more than twenty years. She is the author of *My Name Is Jorge: On Both Sides of the River*, a collection of poems published in both English and Spanish.

John Micklos, Jr., has been an educational journalist for more than twenty years and has written for a wide range of children's and adult publications. His previous books include *Daddy Poems* and *Mommy Poems*.

Jeff Moss has written many children's books, including books of poems. His poem in this collection comes from his book *The Butterfly Jar*.

Grace Nichols, a Caribbean poet, has written a number of poetry books for children. Her poem in *Grandparent Poems* comes from her book *Come On into My Tropical Garden*.

Eileen Spinelli has written several children's picture books and poetry books. Her poem in *Grandparent Poems* comes from her book *Tea Party Today: Poems to Sip and Savor*.

Judith W. Steinbergh's poem for *Grandparent Poems* comes from Myra Cohn Livingston's anthology *Poems for Grandmothers*.

Acknowledgments

Every effort has been made to trace the ownership of each poem included in *Grandparent Poems*. If any errors or omissions have occurred, corrections will be made in subsequent printings, provided the publisher is notified of their existence. We gratefully acknowledge those who granted permission to use the poems that appear in this book.

Bantam Books for "The Picture" from *The Butterfly Jar* by Jeff Moss. Copyright © 1989 by Jeff Moss. Used by permission of Bantam Books, a division of Random House, Inc.

Boyds Mills Press for "Night Walk with Grandpa" from *Under the Breadfruit Tree: Island Poems* by Monica Gunning. Copyright © 1998 by Monica Gunning; "Buddies" from *A Thousand Cousins: Poems of Family Life* by David L. Harrison. Copyright © 1996 by David L. Harrison; "Still" from *Been to Yesterdays: Poems of a Life* by Lee Bennett Hopkins. Copyright © 1995 by Lee Bennett Hopkins; "Summer Twilight" from *Tea Party Today: Poems to Sip and Savor* by Eileen Spinelli. Copyright © 1999 by Eileen Spinelli. Reprinted by permission of Boyds Mills Press.

Children's Book Press for "My Grandma's Songs" from *Laughing Tomatoes and Other Spring Poems* by Francisco X. Alarcón. Reprinted with permission of the publisher, Children's Book Press, San Francisco, CA. Copyright © 1997 by Francisco X. Alarcón.

Curtis Brown, Ltd., for "In Grandpa's House" by Rebecca Kai Dotlich. Copyright © 2002 by Rebecca Kai Dotlich. Reprinted by permission of Curtis Brown, Ltd.

Curtis Brown Ltd., London, for "Granny Granny Please Comb My Hair" from *Come On into My Tropical Garden* by Grace Nichols. Reproduced with permission of Curtis Brown Ltd., London, on behalf of Grace Nichols. Copyright © Grace Nichols 1988.

Dial Books for Young Readers for "Big Mama" from *My Daddy Is a Cool Dude and Other Poems* by Karama Fufuka. Copyright © 1975 by Karama Fufuka; "remembering . . ." from *Something on My Mind* by Nikki Grimes. Copyright © 1978 by Nikki Grimes. Used by permission of Dial Books for Young Readers, a division of Penguin Putnam Inc.

Harcourt for "Grandma Louise's Gingerbread" by Crescent Dragonwagon. From *Food Fight* by Michael J. Rosen. Copyright © 1996 by Crescent Dragonwagon; "Pineapple Surprise" by Nikki Grimes. From *Food Fight* by Michael J. Rosen. Copyright © 1996 by Nikki Grimes. Reprinted by permission of Harcourt, Inc.

Lee & Low Books for "My Granddaddy Is My Daddy Too" by Dinah Johnson. Text copyright © 1997 by Dinah Johnson. From the book *In Daddy's Arms I Am Tall* collection copyright © 1997 by Lee & Low Books. Permission arranged with Lee & Low Books, Inc., New York, NY.

Little, Brown and Company for "Grandmas and Grandpas" from *Fathers, Mothers, Sisters, Brothers* by Mary Ann Hoberman. Text copyright © 1991 by Mary Ann Hoberman. By permission of Little, Brown and Company.

Jane Medina for "I Like to Walk with Grandma" by Jane Medina. Copyright ©1999 by Jane Medina. Reprinted by permission of the author.

John Micklos, Jr., for "Grandpa's Hands," "Grandpa's Sports Car," "I Only Know the Stories," and "I Remember Grandma" by John Micklos, Jr. Copyright © 1999 by John Micklos, Jr.; "When Grandpa Reads to Me" by John Micklos, Jr. Copyright © 2000 by John Micklos, Jr.

Judith W. Steinbergh for "Welcome, Florence" by Judith W. Steinbergh. From *Poems for Grandmothers*, selected by Myra Cohn Livingston. Copyright © 1990 by Judith W. Steinbergh. Reprinted by permission of the author.

Index of Titles and First Lines